Introduction

We tend to assume sweet potato herbs only culture in certain soils or that they are generally harder to take care of than regular potato herbs.

And that stops many gardeners from trying their hand at culturing them.

Sweet Potato Guide: How to Culture

That's a real shame. Sweet potatoes are not only **surprisingly easy to culture however** they are also **a delicious treat**. Much more so than regular potatoes!

White POTATOES vs Sweet POTATOES

White Potatoes		Sweet Potatoes
69	CALORIES	86
2g	PROTEIN	2g
16g	CARBS	20g
2g	FIBER	3g
1g	SUGAR	4g
9mg	CALCIUM	30mg
16mg	SODIUM	55mg
21mg	MAGNESIUM	25mg
407mg	POTASSIUM	337mg
337mg	VITAMIN C	2mg
18ug	FOLATE	11ug
11mg	CHOLINE	12.3mg
8iu	VITAMIN A	14,187iu
13ug	LUTEIN + ZEAZANTHIN	0ug

In this guide, we can share with you **everything you must to famous about culturing sweet potatoes**–the different types of sweet potato herbs, how to herb and culture for them, and more.

Without further ado, let's culture some sweet potatoes!

Varieties of Sweet Potatoes

Supposing you've only rarely dealt with sweet potatoes (either in the garden or the kitchen), you might be under the impression that there's only one type of "yam." however that's not the case.

There are several varieties of sweet potato herbs out there. Let's look at some of the most popular.

The Okinawa

Very popular in Hawaii, the Okinawa sweet potato is a one of a kind treat. What sets this apart from most other sweet potatoes is the vibrant purple color of the flesh inside, which draws a fascinating contrast with the off-white, light violet exterior.

Despite their rich, bright color, Okinawa sweet potatoes are remarkably mild in taste. You'll employ them in a variety of salads or as a replacement for orange types of sweet potatoes.

The Jewel

The Jewel takes us on more familiar ground. This type of sweet potato is far more common. With a dull orange skin, Jewel sweet potatoes are quite versatile. Their flesh is a brighter orange and their taste is not overpoweringly sweet.

Advice: You'll cook Jewel potatoes in many ways–mashed, boiled, roasted, baked.

The Bunch Porto Rico

The Bunch Porto Rico sweet potato herb is, by all accounts, a great option supposing you have a small garden. this doesn't take up much space to grow.

On the outside, the potatoes this produces have a rich copper color. On the inside, we're greeted by a pinkish/yellowy flesh—and a pleasantly sweet taste!

The Hannah

A sweet potato herb with a long history, the Hannah looks remarkably like a 'regular' potato. It's yellowy in color, both on the inside and the outside.

Advice: The Hannah is far denser than your average, orange-tinted sweet potato and does not work well as a replacement for it.

The Satsuma-Imo

As the name suggests, the Satsuma-Imo is a slightly exotic addition to the sweet potato family. this has a very dark purple skin however its flesh is yellow, simply like common potatoes. Its taste, while sweeter than regular potatoes, is surprisingly mild.

The Satsuma-Imo doesn't usually become waterlogged, as many orange-y sweet potatoes do. however being far denser than your average sweet potato, this does not work as a substitute for them either. The Satsuma-Imo is its own thing.

The Beauregard

The Beauregard is the most common type of sweet potato and the one you're most likely to see in stores. Its skin tends to be a dull reddish color (sometimes a little purple). Its bright, orange flesh has by far the sweetest taste of the bunch.

Advice: The Beauregard is not as dense as other sweet potatoes, which do this easier to cook.

The Garnet

The Garnet has a bit of a peculiar skin, which do this simply recognizable–its deep, orange-purple tint stands out pretty much anywhere. This type of sweet potato also has a distinctive, elongated shape.

Inside, we find a deeply orange flesh that is simply one of the most flavored and sweet in existence. Also, the Garnet is exquisitely moist, which do this much easier to cook than most types of sweet potato.

The Centennial

The Centennial sweet potato is one more really common variety. On the inside, this looks remarkably like a carrot.

But don't allow that deceive you. Centennial sweet potatoes give a unique, sweet flavor to most dishes.

The Stokes

The Stokes sweet potato is tricky to identify because it's so similar to the Okinawa. They share that bright purple interior and dull-colored exterior.

One way in which the Stokes potato stands out is through its health profits. It's remarkably rich in antioxidants, and so, an excellent addition to most meals.

The Vardaman

The Vardaman sweet potato stands out through its bright, orange flesh (almost bordering on red, sometimes).

Delectably sweet, it's one more great option for people who don't have a lot of space in their garden—this bush variety potato herb doesn't must much.

How to Culture Sweet Potatoes

Ah, we've reached the tricky part. Simply kidding! There's **nothing to be afraid** of when planting sweet potatoes.

As we've seen, there are many varieties out there, appropriate for every type of soil and garden.

Step one – Assess your planting space

Simply like when you're furnishing a home, you must to be aware of the size of the space you're working with. Otherwise, you risk planting a variety of sweet potato that's too big for your space. So, figure out **how much garden space** you'll **dedicate to culturing sweet potatoes**.

Step two – Buy or Cut Some Sweet Potato Slips

Next, you want to **buy the sweet potato slips**. Sellers usually culture these from other stored sweet potatoes. You mustn't have any trouble finding slips for your chosen type of sweet potato.

Alternatively, you'll **culture sweet potato slips** from an actual sweet potato of your desired variety. Simply slice the potato in two and allow this sit on the planting soil for a while.

Here are some more advices on starting your own sweet potato slips.

Advice: Supposing you're new to all this, buying slips from the store is your best bet to culturing sweet potato herbs without any hassle.

Step 3 – Store the Slips

You may must to **store the slips** for a while before they're ready for planting. Remember, supposing you herb them too early or too late, they may not culture properly.

Advice: Store sweet potato slips in an open space with plenty of light, at **around 70°F (around 20°C)**.

Step 4 – herb Them at the Right Time

Sweet potatoes must to spend quite a bit of time in the ground **(between 90 and 170 days)**, so you'll want to herb them in good time.

Sweet potatoes are **very sensitive to frost**. It's best to herb them **around 3-4 weeks when the last frost** when the soil has had a little time to warm up.

Step 6 – herb Them Right

You'll either herb sweet potatoes in pots or straight in the ground. Supposing employing pots, make sure to get large ones (at least 1-gallon pots for every two slips or so).

Supposing planting sweet potatoes in a pot: *You want to ensure the pot has drainage holes at the bottom. Layer the pot with around 3-4 inches of mulch first, then cover the rest with fertile, planting soil.*

Most people employ planting pots as a preemptive measure, to give the sweet potato a 'head start' and protect this from the danger of frost.

When this danger has passed, it's good to move the sweet potato (should be around 6-12 inches tall now) to the outside.

Plant each strip about **6 inches deep and 12 inches apart from other slips**, then cover with soil. Make little raised mounds where you've planted each slip.

Important: In the first several days, you'll want to water sweet potato herbs well to ensure that they root properly.

Here's a recap of the key steps to planting sweet potatoes.

How to Care For Sweet Potato herbs

Next comes the culturing part. As again, don't worry, this may sound difficult at first, however sweet potatoes are rather easy as you get the hang of them.

Light

Sweet potato herbs like the light, so you want to make sure they get plenty of that. It's recommended that you herb **them in full sun**. however in particularly dry regions, this might be best to find them a spot where they may occasionally get some shade as well.

Soil

You'll want your soil to be as rich in organic matter as possible.

What is organic matter: Organic matter is decaying herb or animal matter. Most commonly, manure. What organic matter does for your herbs is to help strengthen them with whatever they need. For some, it's helping them retain moisture, while for others, this improves drainage.

A trick many gardeners employ is to spread black plastic over the soil, to help the soil warm up. With sweet potatoes, you might consider **planting them in raised soil**, which again, serves to protect them from frost.

Watering

As the first several crucial days have passed, you no longer must to water them so heavily. They've probably taken root by now and too much water possibly detrimental.

About **an inch of water every week** should be fine. As they've taken root, sweet potato herbs may tolerate dry soil surprisingly well. Try to keep them moist however avoid flooding them.

Important: Make sure to give your sweet potato herbs a breather the last 3 or so weeks before harvesting. Watering in that period may cause the mature tubing to split. That may seriously affect your harvest!

Fertilizing

A good idea is to put down some compost before you herb the sweet potatoes. It's usually alright to **add fertilizer every month or so** (but don't overdo it!). When choosing your fertilizer, look for one that is **high in phosphate**.

Advice: Stop fertilizing about the same time you stop watering the sweet potato herbs before harvesting. Anywhere from two to 4 weeks should be fine, depending on your type of potato/climate combo.

Temperature

As again, sweet potatoes are **really sensitive to frost**. They Dont like the cold and won't culture in cold temperatures. So, when you herb them outside, you want to wait until the soil temperature has warmed up to around 60°F (around 15°C).

Sweet potato herbs must a temperature **between 60° and 85° F (15 to 30°C)** to culture in the soil. They also require an climate temperature of up to 95°F (35°C).

Warning: Don't herb your sweet potatoes too early in the spring, otherwise, they won't culture as they should.

Pests and Diseases

While your potatoes grow, you want to make sure other creatures don't get to them before you do.

Wireworms, mice, and root-knot nematodes are your most common worries when culturing sweet potatoes.

You want to **have a soil rich in good microorganisms** that discourages the growth of harmful bacteria. You'll also must some form of pest control, to ward off mice or other above-ground critters.

Advice: Practice crop rotation–don't herb your sweet potato herbs in the same spot each year. This can discourage pests.

Then we have the diseases your sweet potato patch is exposed to—Stem rot, white blisters, and fungal leaf diseases are all common.

You'll ward many of these off by ensuring you **buy high-quality, certified, disease-free sweet potato slips**. As for the rot, you'll keep that at bay by not overwatering.

Advice: Hoe the soil occasionally, to ensure that the vines of the herb culture as they should.

How to Harvest Sweet Potatoes

Usually, sweet potato herbs are ready to be harvested as their leaves start to yellow. however you'll leave them in the ground for longer, to increase the sweet potatoes vitamin content.

As you do decide it's harvest time, here's how to do it:

1. Harvest sweet potatoes on a sunny, dry day.
2. Begin digging out the tubers however beware that sweet potato tubers culture close to the surface and are tender. Dig gently!

3. As you've properly dug out the tubers, leave them to dry in the sun (up to several hours). Make sure to keep them safe from pests and scroungers.
4. When drying the tubers, you want to store them in a well-ventilated, hot area (around 85-90°F/30-35°C) for around two weeks or so.
5. When this period, your sweet potatoes have been cured and you'll store them a colder place (around 55°F/13°C) with high humidity. Supposing properly tended to, they possibly stored for several months.

Here are some more potato harvesting advices.

Sweet Potato herbs FAQ

May you culture sweet potatoes from a sweet potato?

Yes. Simply get a sweet potato and either cut this in half or in several large chunks. Sprouts can begin culturing on your sliced sweet potato. As the sprout is 5-6 inches tall, remove this gently and herb it.

How many sweet potatoes do you get from one plant?

One sweet potato herb can generally yield at least one pound of sweet potatoes or around 10 average-size potatoes. however this varies from herb to herb and from garden to garden.

What is a good companion herb for sweet potatoes?

Most commonly, root vegetables make for excellent sweet potato companions. Beets and roots are good ideas, as are bush beans.

May I herb a sweet potato from the grocery store?

Of course. You'll simply from store-bought sweet potatoes that can then yield several sweet potato herbs. Look for organic sweet potatoes, however any store-bought potatoes should do simply fine.

Not Simply Potatoes however Sweet Potatoes

Sweet potatoes are easy to culture and really aren't such a demanding plant—at all! What you must to remember about sweet potato herbs is they are **sensitive to frost, must space to grow, and like the sun**.

With these three things in mind, there's no reason why this time next year, you mustn't have a full sweet potato batch simply sitting somewhere in the house, ready for the cooking.

Made in the USA
Las Vegas, NV
23 December 2021

39305887R00015